Reflections

ROBERT W. WHITE

 FriesenPress

One Printers Way
Altona, MB R0G 0B0
Canada

www.friesenpress.com

Author & Photographer: Rosemary M. Kanigan

ISBN
978-1-03-919663-6 (Hardcover)
978-1-03-919662-9 (Paperback)
978-1-03-919664-3 (eBook)

1. POETRY / CANADIAN

Distributed to the trade by The Ingram Book Company

Contents

Special Section: Golf, Family, Friends, Special Occasions *

My Lady Rose

My Lady Rose, my wife
A blossom so true and dear
Together through life we shared
Our hopes and dreams and fears.

A blossom so fresh
When she came to the ranch
A girl of my dreams
The one I would keep
My Lady Rose.

Three blooms did come
From My Lady Rose.
She gave them life and love
Only a mother knows
And they grew to an image of
My Lady Rose.

Our many years together
Through times both bad and good
Few men could be so lucky
To pick a bloom of such beauty
As my Lady Rose.

My Hat

I was born a cryin' and squawkin'
Cute as a little bug's ear.
The part I found quite shockin'
Was the smack applied to my rear.

My ma was a school teachin' cowgirl
You know I'm thankful for that
But the worst part of the turmoil
Was they forgot to put on my hat.

The three-cornered pants I could tolerate
The booties and leggings were great
The bonnet was cute, but I hastened to add
I wanted a cowboy hat just like my dad.

So, I kept the pressure on Mother
As I roped the old tom cat
I knew that sooner or later
She'd break down and buy me a hat.

One day I heeled my Ma
As she was goin' about her chores
It took her by real surprise
When she was laid out on the floor.

I tied her hind legs together
Put the piggin' around her spurs
I grabbed the hand that was reachin' for me
Did two wraps and a hitch in a blur.

As I stood and looked at my captive
And realized just what I'd done
Pa appeared at the door, saw Ma on the floor
Said, "Yup he sure is my son."

He scooped me up and said with a grin,
"It's time we went into town
We'll get you that hat, shiny and black
With a wide brim and a crease in the crown."

This story's as true as I'm talkin' to you
Just ask the old tom cat
He'll raise his right paw, say I tied up my Ma
The day that I got my black hat.

The Irrigator

In the quiet morning of a midsummer day
The farmer rises early to irrigate his hay
With shovel in hand and a horse that will stand
Till the water is set for a day.

The irrigator's job to build ditches that leak
Yet still bring water from the faraway creek.
From the top of the field, he would set it just right
Before the flies and mosquitoes awoke and took flight.
When the sun came up to caress the tall grass
He'd better be done before the bugs could harass.

That morning at breakfast the phone started to ring
That smooth talkin' salesman said, "I've got a sure thing.
It's called aluminum pipe, and it comes with a pump.
Stick one end in the creek and fire it up.
You can measure the water for each acre of land
Stand and admire a magnificent stand."

The part we missed in his communication
Was the dollars it cost for the whole operation.
The risers and sprinklers and gasket you'd need
Sure, helped the hay crop but made your wallet bleed.

Then you'd struggle and strain to make the pipe fit
Unplug the nozzles and your eye would get hit
Right in your face was the start of the shower
Then right in your belly with all its power.

The bike you now rode instead of a horse
Wouldn't start, so now you really could curse.
Mad as a hornet and soaked to the skin
Then as you looked up that salesman drove in.

"Havin' trouble I see, but I know how you feel,
For a bit more money we'll put on some wheels.
A brand-new wheel line is just what you need
Why the cost will be mere chicken feed!"

So now you can see the pipes are on wheels
It's no longer diesel but hydro that steals.
The profits are gone, the banker makes me grovel
I long for my horse and my long-handled shovel.

Snoring

When I wake up in the dark of night
There's a sound that makes me wonder
Is it a freight train shuntin' cars
Or maybe just distant thunder.

Sometimes it's real melodious
Like music in your ears
Other times it's really frightening
Like an eighteen-wheeler changin' gears.

A pause, a deep breath, now it sounds crisper
As you lay and begin to wonder
It returns like a rumble of far-off thunder.

Now we've been married forty years
Plus, a couple more.
It's hard to believe as I lay there
My wife has started to snore.

She'll gag and choke and wake with a start
Turn towards me and say, from the bottom of her heart
"I didn't sleep very well, had a restless night"
Every time you turned over the covers took flight.
Don't sleep on your back and there's one thing more
I'd sure sleep better if YOU didn't snore.

Morning

When you crawl out in the morning
And the world is cold and still
The clouds are low and threatening
But the sun shines through on the hill.

It sparkles on the snow-covered trees
With the sky of blue above
There's the promise of a beautiful day
In this western land we love.

When your old horse knickers as you go feed
As if to say, "You're a little late
But that's okay give me my oats and hay
I'll be ready and waitin' at the gate."

The smell of coffee perkin'
And the eggs are fryin' too
Greets you as you come back in
And go through the list of the jobs to do.

There's calves to feed and cows to check
And the corral rail to fix
Tag the newborns, clean up the wreck in pen number six
The front tire's flat on the tractor.

The bull's bellerin' and buttin' the gate
There's so many jobs to do out there
Some of 'em will just have to wait
I'll just sit a spell and watch the sun
Warm up this magical land
And thank God for choosin' this one
To be one of the few, an old cowboy hand.

This life's disappearin' at a frightful pace
It was a golden time in the human race
The old cowboys are almost gone
But the legends remain in words and song.

The Little Outhouse

My Grandpa he was an industrious gent
A man of not many words
So, it followed through that the outhouse he built
He didn't use too many boards.

That little house that stands out back
Had a really faithful clientele
Oh, there was room enough to contemplate
And watch the world go by as well.

There was room enough for business
But you ducked when you entered the door
Because if you didn't and hit your head
You sure wound up on the floor.

The floor plan was simple, three feet square
Room enough but none to spare
One hole to sit upon to ease your pain
Worn smooth from use again and again.

There were cracks in the walls from lumber green
You could sit and squint and not be seen
But winter's winds blew through those cracks
So, you didn't loiter before making tracks.

Be sure to duck as you exit the door
Or your head would ache forever more
The outhouse brings memories forever stuck
When in a hurry I forgot to duck.

Mother

Legends abound in this great land
Of the deeds and victories of many great men
But the untold stories of suffering, passion, and pain
Of the women who helped with each hard-fought gain

Partners in the vision to benefit all
They came west with their men when duty called
From the mist of the past and the Indian wars
Shines the courage of Hannah, as a prisoner she bore

The death of her captors for freedom's gain
From the founding fathers came Maria Jane
Strong willed and God fearing, raised her family alone
As tragedy struck her husband down

The call came for Mary to mother this clan
The far west it beckoned, her and her man
Through daughter Rhoda, the spirit came through
A rancher's wife, a pioneer true

Only names from the past, but the mothers of sons
Who tamed our great land and forged it into one
Canada, our country, like no other
Our thanks to the men and the women we call
"MOTHER"

The Old Mailbox

At the gate to the ranch there stands an old friend
The battered old mailbox, with a hole in the end
It has stood there for years, through storms, wind, and rain
Held many memories, some happiness, tears and pain.

It was a mile and a half from the house to the gate
We often left early, didn't want to be late
The mailman could come, maybe at ten, eleven, or two
If you were lucky to meet him you got some visiting too.

Old George brought the news
Some gossip and stories, sometimes true
He'd say I haven't got much time, gotta go on through
Two hours later he was still talkin' to you.

Finally, he'd say, "I really have to go"
Crank up the old Chev and head through the snow
You'd look through the mail, parcels, papers, and such
A half a sack full, I was glad there wasn't that much.

Jump on your horse and with a flip of its tail
Race with the dog and that sack of mail
Old W.W. put up that shiny new box,
When the homestead was young and rough.

He tamped in the post and heaped it with rocks,
Painted on this name, said, "That's good enough"
He built up his ranch with his son Tom,
Rhoda became a teacher, Will a sawbones

Ruby married young the oldest of four
The mailbox was the link in the days of yore
The weather's still tough on that old tin box,
Rainstorms and cold, the winds make it rock

In the forties a new name covered up Shaw.
Frank and Rhoda WHITE, my ma and Pa.
We painted our name on that rusty old box
Tightened our belt, and pulled up our socks

We built a big ranch out of what Grampa left
"WHITECROFT" the result, one of the best
That old mailbox has sure stood the test
Through heat and cold, it's outlived the rest.

We painted on "WHITECROFT" all shiny and new
But the wind and rain have washed that off too.
We moved that old box when the ranch was sold
Still part of the family, but it still stands in the cold

That lonely old sentinel, a link with the past
I hear the ghosts calling whenever I pass
For ninety years it's put up a good fight
Now the name on the side is just plain "WHITE."

The Old Buggy

That broken old buggy down by the well
If it could talk it would have a story to tell
Of horses and sleighs and bygone days
Pull up a stump and hear what it says.

"My big red wheels and shiny leather seat
Were the envy of everyone that we would meet
That fancy trotter between my shaves
We could out-pace 'em all and not look back.

That young couple that brought me took such pride
They'd shine and polish me before each ride.
Soon children came and I was too small
So, they changed to a wagon to take them all.

I was just used Sundays or on special days
Soon along came a doctor and took me away
We travelled the country for miles each week
Even delivered a baby down by the creek.

From gunshots to bruises we treated then all
The Doc and I answered each call.
Soon the Doc bought a car, retirement was ahead
He carefully parked me out in the shed.

For years I waited, neglected and old
Then a familiar voice said," I'm glad you're not sold"
My original owner, bent over and grey
Put me in his pickup and took me away.

He restored me that winter, with much loving care
Took me out in the spring hitched to a high steppin' mare
He showed his grandchildren, with obvious pride
How he took their grandma for her Sunday ride.

This family is proud of my part in their past
If you want to hear more, just pause and ask.

The Old Saddle

It was one of those mornings in August
When the air was cool and still
An' I stood there in the barn door
And watched the sun creep down the hill.

It was one of those magical moments
That just seem to happen now and again
It's hard to tell someone they happen
They think you're fickle or fey.

I heard a small sound behind me
And I turned very slowly to see
The dust sparkles rise from the saddle
My grandpa had left it for me.

It sat on a bar in the corner
In the stall where he kept his horse
See, that part of the barn is "off limits"
Kind of a shrine to the man in my past.

Now this man wasn't really a cowboy
In the strictest sense of the word
Oh, he could get a job done
Put a stray back into the herd.

He had no trophies or buckles to brag on
Just a lifetime of struggle and strain
He was tough like that old saddle
That showed all the years in its grain.

I could feel his presence that morning
I knew he was there watching me
Now that saddle creaked as he mounted
The dust particles rose in the sun
I could hear his voice as he shouted
"Come on, let's get this job done."

The Bra

Y'see I've never been much for shoppin'
In fact, I try to stay away from town
And except when shippin' time comes
I ain't too easily found.
But the day came when I had to go
So, I left the kids with Ma
But before I left, she asked me
Could I pick her up a bra?
Well without thinkin' I said sure
How tough could that job be
I bent down to kiss her
Said I'll be back by three.
Well, when I'd done the things, I needed to
I started to regret ever offerin' to buy that thing
And I started workin' up a sweat
I crossed the street to the lady's shop
With my hat pulled over my eyes
I couldn't take any chances
See I didn't want to get recognized
Well, I walked right up to the salesclerk
Didn't even hem or haw
Told the lady straight out
"Ma'am I'm here to buy a bra."
From behind I heard some snickering
So, I turned around to see
At least fifteen women gawkin'
And a grinnin' straight at me
"What style would you be looking for?"
Well, I just scratched my head
I'd only seen one kind before

"Thought bras was bras," I said
She gave me a disgusted look
Said, "Sir, that's where you are wrong
Come with me," I heard her say
And like a dog I tagged along.
She took me down this alley
Where them bras was on display
I thought my jaw would hit the floor
When I saw the lingerie!
There's all these different styles and shapes
Like I'd not seen before
Figured I'd go crazy for I left that women's store
There's bras you'd wear for eighteen hours
And bras that cross yer heart
Bras that lift and separate
An' that was just the start
Heck there's bras that make you feel
Like you weren't wearin' one at all
And bras that you can train in
To start out when yer small.
Well, I finally made up my mind, picked a black and lacy one
Told the lady to just bag it up, I figured I was done
But then she asked me for the size
I didn't hesitate
I knew them measurements by heart
I said, "Six and seven eights."
"Six and seven eights," she said,

"Surely that's not right."
"Well yes ma'am, I'm positive,
see I measured them last night."
I thought that she'd go in shock
Must a took her by surprise
When I told her my wife's bust
Was the same as my hat size.
"That's what I used to measure with, I figured it was fair
But well if I'm wrong, I'm sorry ma'am."
That just drew another stare.
By now a crowd has gathered
They are all a crackin' up.
When the lady asked to see my hat
So, she could measure for the cup.
When she finally had it figured
I just give the gal her pay
Turned to leave the store,
Tipped my hat and said good day.
My wife had heard this story fore
I even made it home
See she had talked to fifteen women
Who had called her on the phone.
And she was still a laughin'
But by then I didn't care.
Cuz now she don't ask, and I don't shop
For no more women's wear.

Bras and Saddle Horns

Now a lady came out to the ranch
And we put her on a horse
And this old Western saddle
Well, it had a horn of course
Now a lady's bra and saddle horns
They don't often match
And if you get hung up on one
You're bound to get a scratch
Now she stepped up on that old horse
With lots of grace and style
But when I saw what got hooked on that horn
Well, I just had to stop and smile
She's a tuggin' and she's a pullin'
But in spite of what she tries
She's hung up by her bra strap
She's hung out to dry
She's wigglin' and she's squirmin'
And then she starts to curse
She said, "It's harder on my boobers
Than to teach a kid to nurse!"

So, the next time she comes to the ranch
To ride out in the morn
I'll get an old English saddle
Cause they don't have a horn
Now she can ride the buckskin horse
Or she can ride the roan
Or she can just like bounce along
And leave her bra at home
Now she's a busty gal you see
She's a shakin' every ounce
And every time the horse comes down
Things really bounce
She's bouncing on down the hill
The old horse he looks back
You'd swear she had a grizzly bear
A tied there in a sack.

So, girls before you go on the trail
So, things will work out right
Just get a roll of friction tape
And wrap yourself real tight
I'm not tellin' you to hide 'em
Or keep 'em out of sight
But to save yourself some trouble
Just tuck 'em in real tight
See boobs they are a gift from God
At that we shouldn't scorn
But they belong inside a bra
Not on a saddle horn.

Mac Park Golf

This poem came about after playing many games of golf with a group of retired school bus drivers and my brother-in-law, Jack Brady. I often call him "Pappy"—he is thirteen years older than me and I have known him all my life.

On Tuesdays it's coffee and on to Mac Park
For nine holes of golf, we all leave our mark.
We practice a bit before we begin
We all listen to Pappy and let the words sink in.

Keep your eye on the ball and swing right through
Well watch where it goes when you don't swing true.
Pappy's words will haunt you as you listen to this
Where did I go wrong, I went through the list

I held the club tight, like he told me to do
The backswing was slow, measured and true.
Pappy's words came back to me again and again
"Keep your eye on the ball and swing rite through"

Down came the club, hit the ball with a crack
It flew to the left, hit the fence with a smack.
Flew to the right, hit a tree on the trunk,
Rolled down the green and went in with a plunk

We all just stood there, nearly struck dumb
We had just witnessed a "hole in one."
Those fateful words echoed, that we all knew were true
"Keep your eye on the ball and swing right through."

If you make a mistake, Murphy may step in
Put something in the way to make the ball spin.
In this game of golf, it can go to or fro'
Pappy's words may haunt you, "You just never know."

Goin' For a Swim

One really hot day in two thousand and one
We went to the lake for some cool water fun
Now us retired ranchers, we're showin' our years
But as recycled teenagers we just use lower gears.

When we got to the lake there were people everywhere
So, to launch our boat took a great deal of care
It slid into the water just like cutting cheese
And I parked the truck up under some trees.

But gettin' aboard was quite a show
We finally got settled and well under way
To a quiet little spot in a secluded small bay
There was an old dock pulled up on the shore
A good place to swim, we'd been there before.

Now the lake's a bit low, the dock's on a slope
She said, "Just drive right on,
I'll get off with the rope."
Now my girl's not as nimble as she used to be.

As soon as she stood on that dock I could see
Her feet started to slide on the slime under water
She stood for a moment and started to totter
She turned real fast to grab on the boat
But it had started back as it still was afloat.

She grabbed with both hands, but was leanin' to port
Her feet slid on the boards as she looked for support
She stretched right out nearly seven feet tall
The end was inevitable, she started to fall.

There was a mighty splash as she landed with grace
Mad as a wet hen, I could tell from her face
I was in trouble I knew it, couldn't stop the guffaw
But she didn't think it was funny, no not at all.

She floats like a cork, her hair wasn't even wet
As she swam to the dock and crawled onto the deck
It was lucky for me I was still on the boat.
She'd have drowned me for sure if she'd got hold of my throat.

As my laughter subsided, she started to grin
"You did that on purpose to watch me fall in"
"Not on your life, I wouldn't do that to you
But it was awful funny from this point of view."

So now there's a change in our little boat crew
She does the drivin' and tells *me* what to do.

—July 25, 2001

Shirley

The mechanics and drivers of "seventy-three"
Are gathered together to honor Shirley
She's heard all our jokes and tales of woe
Of intolerable kids and buses that won't go.

She's at her desk every day, sometimes alone
The radio in one hand and then there's the phone
She's typing up trips and adding up gas
Then there's the boss chewin' her ass.

She looks after fifty guys, each drivin' a rig
The only steno I know with a harem this big
When we go for the keys at the start of each trip
She's there at her desk with a smile on her lips.

We'll miss you Shirley, for retirement's your fate
With the approach of that magic date
Reflect on a job that you did very well
You've left us with memories, you've cast a spell.

May you have many years, your stories to tell
Enjoy your retirement, we all wish you well.

—June 25, 2001

The Red-Necked Roan

Now every cowboy has some memories
Of calves that he has saved from the storm
Usually, one stands out from all the rest
It's beaten the odds and passed the test
Like the one to be known as the red-necked roan.

Why I remember like yesterday the day that she was born
It was cold and snowy, one hell of a storm
One day in February, checkin' those that had arrived
Prayin' to God that they all had survived
Like the one to be known as the red-necked roan.

She was layin' there frozen in the pasture by the storm
Behind her dead mother, this little calf that was roan
She had little short ears on a big ugly head
With white spots on her rump, she looked nearly dead
This little orphan calf known as the red-necked roan.

We packed her to the barn, put her under a light
She soon came to life and right full of fight
She was determined to live, defiance was there
A foster mother was found to give her special care
This little orphan calf called the red-necked roan.

That fall when she came home all sassy and slick
That roan with the red neck is one that we'll keep.
She continued to thrive, in a year was a mom
A little bull calf, he was his mother's son
This cow that was known as the red-necked roan.

To tag her new calf wasn't much fun
Sneak up behind, tag it and run
If it made a sound, she was on the attack
You had to scramble for safety upon the hay rack
A dedicated mother, that red-neck roan.

The years went by one by one, till they added up to ten
She got pretty independent, was the first one out of the pen
She knew the date to come to the gate to go to the
mountain range
"Get out of my way," she used to say. "You follow for a change"
This ornery cow we all knew now as the red-necked roan.

Next year's calf was a heifer, the first she ever had
It was weak and small; we tried our all but soon it lay dead
We turned her out with the dry cows, she went to the
mountain instead
A summer of leisure was her due, the old cow whose head was red
We all knew it was due, the cow called the red-necked roan.

When I think back of all the tracks, I followed that cursed cow
Through barbed wire and brush most often in a rush I now
wonder how
She seemed to delight in makin' me fight, but she always got
her way
I swore that I'd get even if it took to my dyin' day
I'd beat that hide on either side of that red-necked roan.

It was a hard decision when she came home all alone
For this was the last summer of the cow, the red-necked roan
But I made her hide into leather that became my favourite chaps
So, she rode with me every day and maybe the Lord will perhaps
Grant her a pasture she can use all alone
This crop-eared, bobtail cow, known as the red-necked roan.

—2001

The Ballad of Jack Gillespie

A very good friend, who was adopted as an infant, finally found his birth family (parents deceased) after much searching. He now has many relatives all over the country and is enjoying himself with his newfound family.

There's a guy named Frank we've known for years
Worked for B.C. Tel amid hisses and cheers.
He came from Thunder Bay as a very young fellow
Adopted by parents both caring and mellow.

He grew up in Kamloops did Frank and his pipe
The bane of his teachers from Potter to Wright.
He married Doreen from the country she came
Settled down on Nicola, grew tobacco by the lane.

Two girls came along, Susan and Pat
They moved to Dominion Street soon after that.
A brand-new house with a mortgage for years
He paid all the bills and had money for beer.

They fished all the lakes around Lac Le Jeune
Bought a lot with a cabin where he still plays those tunes.
He retired from Tel at fifty-five years
Helped Doreen bake her cakes and started changin' gears.

He's handling retirement with style and grace
Goes south every year for a nice change of pace.
He started to wonder from what roots did he come
Searched 'round Thunder Bay for Daddy and Mom.

Relations turned up beneath every stone
Both in the north and the south and closer to home.
The search for his roots went a long way back
Now Gillespie is the name, and he answers to JACK.

Cattle Drive

A cattle drive is a big event, it will stir your heart and fears
Whether it is the modern kind or one from a hundred years
Many of us were born on the land, some transplanted there
We've shared the strife, lived the life, we're here because we care.

We honour those who came before to tame this wild land
Those men and women from our past, sometimes it's hard
to understand
But we all share in some small way the spirit that drove them on
They fought each battle as it came, "By God I'm glad they won."

They packed up their families, left all that they knew
To cross our great country, to start out fresh and new
They fought distance, heat and mud, mosquitoes, flies and flood
The way west was quite a test, some stories were written
in blood.

So, we are all descendants of that mighty crew
Who came and built this land of ours, they had a job to do
And what a land they've passed to us, I hope we've done the same
For the kids who follow us and choose to play the game.

For they, like us, will place their trust in the land that kept us all
And leave a better world behind, before the final call
So, ride with pride, you modern cowboys, into the coming dawn
Keep the memories, spirit, and tradition alive of those who were
here and are gone.

—July 14, 2001

A Cowboy's Memories

The old cowboy stood out by the corral
Leanin' against the top rail.
Watchin' the sunset and those wispy clouds
Lost in the memories of a lifelong trail.

Back as a kid, the memories were dim
Ridin the pony his grandpa gave to him.
That little mare could run like a blur
Bareback he rode, stuck on like a burr.

His first workin' horse, a son of his mare
Mostly Cayuse and tough, they made quite a pair.
Many a cow he chased up those hills
That horse was a worker, there were no frills.

A tear crossed his cheek, and he brushed it away
He could see in the clouds his horses from yesterday.
Their eyes were clear and their ears alert
He was sure they had spotted his old red shirt.

That heavenly pasture with the grass so tall
Waving in the wind with just a hint of fall.
A cloud crossed the sun as it started to fade
This vision of heaven he just wouldn't trade.

The memories of his horses, each one was a friend
The memories of trails, lookin' round the next bend.
The sun it was fading, the vision grew dim
"Thank you, Lord, for lookin' after them."

—2001

Lou

As a man gets a little older, he's not travellin' at such a rate
He can sit on a stump and ruminate about the choices he's made.
How life has pushed him here and there, some of the deals
were great
But the one decision he wouldn't change was when he picked out
a mate.

An ex-Saskatchewan farmer bought the ranch just down the road
He'd been living in the city, but that life was a heavy load.
Now this fella had two daughters, their schoolin' years
were through
A slick young guy from the city snagged the one that was known
as Lou.

The July 1st dance was goin' full swing, we were havin' a hell of
a time
When a friend introduced me to Rose, now I can't remember
the line
I used to get her to dance with me, but I sure remember that girl.
The rest of the year was just a blur, things were in a whirl
We set up a home back on the ranch, what else could I do.

Along about Christmas time I realized my sister-in-law was Lou;
Now Lou was leery of cowboys, she thought we were brash
and loud.
She'd let me get close once in a while as long as there was a crowd
Like tamin' a filly out in the corral, it was a sizable job
But after a while she come to accept the brother-in-law
called Rob.

Soon the two sisters were mothers, they decided to take a chance
Diana and Lou and Uncle Stan too, left the city to live on
Dad's ranch.
One burden to bear, Sandy's death we did share, some answers
we all did seek.

With jobs here and there, none could compare
with the one he found at Cache Creek.
Soon Christina was chosen to share their life and fill their
empty hearts
For many years they lived their life on the banks of the Bonapart
Sixteen Mile became their home beside old Ninety-Seven.

Through the years they built their dream, their little bit of heaven
The girls are gone, they're on their own with help from Mom
and Dad
And grandson Regan makes these times the best they ever had.

The golden years are here at last, retirement is their lot
They're havin' fun with all the toys that Uncle Stanley bought.
It took a lot to tame that filly, she's still skittish that is true
I finally came to realize I'm lucky to have a sister-in-law like LOU.

Stanley

We are gathered here tonight to honour our friend Stan
To help him pass a milestone on his journey cross our land
He was born in 1930, Alice and Lee were Mom and Dad
Bill and Lloyd also came along, thank God that's all they had.

They started in the Okanagan, an apple picker he would be
Soon they left for Vancouver to live down by the sea
They played a little hockey did these brothers three
Tormented many a schoolteacher as they lived down by the sea.

Through the years they parted, went their separate ways
But kept in touch especially on these special days.

Now Stan he drove a truck, that's where he met fair Lou
He married her, the lucky girl, now they were two.
Diana and Sandy did arrive, but this was not to be
With Sandy gone Chris was chosen to complete the family.

Many jobs he did do from manual work to string musician
But early on decided to become an electrician
30 years at Ashcroft he kept the schools tickin'
Made many friends along the way, of retirement he was thinkin'.

Now in his truck and trailer he travels far and wide
Across the land, north and south, with Lou worryin' by his side
Flat tires and blown motors he takes them all in stride
Pats Ol' Betsy on the fender, says, "Come on Lou, let's ride."

Now down the road of life, he's come a long fair way
Also became a grandfather when Regan came this way.
Now 70 years is a long, long time to try to get your own way
But we're all here tonight Stan to wish you "HAPPY BIRTHDAY."

Al and Dee

In nineteen hundred and fifty-two
Two young people said "I do"
They promised love and trust in every way
To each other 'til their death someday.

Alan and Delores, you have come a long way
Together you've travelled to reach this day
The boy trumpet player from Old Burnaby
And the shy Dutch girl from the Fraser Valley.

You had quite a time to catch this clown
To make him behave and then settle down
To share your life God gave you two girls
Alanna and Dallas, two wonderful pearls.

The Cariboo beckoned; you answered the call
Going back to the land was tough for you all
On that little homestead near Buffalo Creek
The girls grew strong, not mild and meek.

With farming and logging, the years flew past
The school bus arrived to get the girls to class
With Al as the driver, they were sure to get through
Cold, snow, or mud didn't bother this crew.

Then came a move out to Monte Lake
Another school bus was a job that he'd take
For twenty-five years he travelled that road
To deliver each day his precious load.

Now Dee, close to town, stretched her own wings
She worked in an office and painted nice things
You can see her talent in the pictures around
Quiet and serene, not like the trumpet's sound.

Now Al is a collector of some renown
Other's cast-offs are treasures found
Cars and trucks, bikes and boats
Musical instruments, beehives and bolts.

Old neighbours and friends you made in the past
All came here today to wish you the best
May you have many more years and look back with pride
On your life and your daughters, your wife by your side.

—2002

The Grannie Escapade

Listen real close as this tale is told
Remember these events as they unfold.
A lull in the haying gave time for this trip
To the north country, to visit sonny and his chick.

Grandpa and Grandma and Great Grandpa too
And two Great Grannies made up this crew.
With five in the car there were lots of laughs
They all changed places when they stopped for gas.

The visit was fine. Granddaughter was great
They started home Sunday, they couldn't be late.
They were zipping along, everything was just so
When one great grannie said, "I've just got to go."

"It's a hundred kilometers to the next rest stop
I can't wait that long, I'll surely blow my top.
Find a side road, I'll duck into the trees
Oh please, please hurry I'm weak in the knees."

Now the power of suggestion is pretty unique
Soon all in the car needed to leak.
A side road was found, they turned off real quick
The doors flew open as they abandoned the ship.

For Grandpa it was no problem, he just leaned by a tree
Mother Nature had endowed him with the right anatomy.
But ladies, they are different, I say with some tact,
Without modern facilities it is a balancing act.

Now three grannies with bare fannies is a sight to behold
It's in the interest of science that this story is told.
But Murphy lurked behind a birch in the northern bush
With three grannies bare he could only stare and give a
little push.

Now the centre of gravity changes with the passing of the flood
As one great grannie soon found out as she sat down in the mud.
Soon the sound of laughter floated on the breeze
As the second great grannie fell down upon her knees.

Now Murphy is persistent no matter how he feels
The third grannie he got too, but she just wet her heels.
Great Grandpa was embarrassed, he sat there looking blank
See, he had no problems he had a bigger tank.

Soon dignity restored, as they cleaned off all the mud
Three grannies caught out in the bush, victims of the flood.
Now the moral of this story will make you stop and think
The distance that you travel is measured by how much coffee that
you drink.

—August 30, 2002

The Trip of '01

We were well into winter of two thousand and one
We thought we'd go south and chase the sun
Play some golf and see the sights
Get away from the cold, the snow and ice.

Got some American bucks and hit the road
We were travelling light, just a small load
We crossed over the border; we were well on our way
Got to Moses Lake and found a place to stay.

Next morn it was foggy with some snow and ice
From Pendelton on it wasn't very nice
La Grand and Baker it was tough all the way
We made it to Boise; it was enough for us this day.

On to Twin Falls through the fog and the gloom
We got there OK. I was glad it was noon.
We put gas in the car, we were nearly halfway
Out of the fog into a bright sunny day.

The motor was tickin' as we drove along
It was tryin' to tell us something was wrong.
To Jackpot, Wells, and Ely that night
We stayed in the Jailhouse; it was all right.

The tickin' was worse as we drove along
We stopped at the Alamo; we knew something was wrong
There was nothing to do but keep goin' along
With Las Vegas in sight came the end of the song.

BCCA dispatched a truck, a Manhattan man picked us up
The Speedway hotel became our home for a week
They put in a new motor, our bank sprung a leak
A phone call from Gillespie gave our spirits a lift
It was on to Palm Springs and a week for a gift.

They fed us like kings and gave us a bed
And just let us talk and empty our head
It gave us some hope that things aren't all black
We're blessed to have friends like Doreen and Jack.

Velma and Jack 60 Years

A toast to my sister and her husband Jack
Married sixty years they go a long way back
They met in the halls of old Richmond High
My shy older sister and this debonair guy.

Dan Cupid was there and did his work well
He soon had them both under his spell
Vel soon brought him home to meet her mom and dad
Rhoda and Frank took a shine to this lad.

He soon started work at old Pacific Meat
Vel became a teacher which was kind of neat
Soon war clouds arose, the future looked grim
"The heck with it, Dad, I'm going to marry him."

The war it ended, the boys they came home
To wives and children, they had left all alone
His wife and son waited there on the ranch.
"The rancher and cowboy I'll be, just give me a chance."

Soon Brenda was born, a sister for Barry
The road it was icy, the trip home it was scary.
All went well, 'til that fateful day
When Grampa Frank was taken away.

The family carried on with Mom at the head
Whitecroft was formed and the family it spread
Brenda and Barry were soon on their own
Bringing children and grandchildren into the fold.

So, Velma and Jack you've reason to be proud
A great family you've raised, they are quite a crowd
Sixty years ago, you had no thought of this day
Of the family you have gathered. We honour you today!

—April 4, 2002

Sorting Cows

Sorting cows with Steiners
Is an experience like no other
For it is quite traumatic
When you take the calves from their mothers.

I happened by one frosty day
When they were getting ready to ship
I stood and watched for a little while
And decided I could help a bit.

A sore right knee had slowed me down
But I thought I could work a gate
But one gate sags and the other drags
And where they meet the fence is weak.

"Just take 'em easy," Ueli said as they milled around the pen
"We'll get that nervous one when she comes around again"
But she had years of experience, and her eye was red with hate
You guys are surely dreamin', I ain't goin' out that gate.

She'd snort and hide and duck behind as she went around the pen
Around, she went, five more times, it never seemed to end
"Watch her Brrrenda," Ueli cried, "she's goin' to try it alone"
"Watch her yourself," she mumbled as she stumbled on a stone.

Those thousand pounds of damn mad cow
Was intent on breaking free
She braked at the last second as I slammed the gate shut tight
About then I began to wonder if I'd make it home tonight.

"I've pulled your calf the last three years" I heard Ueli say
"My disposition suffers, my arms are getting' sore
You're going to be hamburger soon
At the nearest Coopers store."

Now she was real excited and loose as cows can be
A gale of shit went flyin' by, her tail was swingin' free
She was blowin' snot with every jump as she saw another gate
"Open it wide," Ueli cried and Brenda gave a heave

It didn't swing like all gates should, but a crack was all she'd need
In there with all the other culls, she thought that she was free.

Now that job's done, we'll sort the calves
This ought to be a snap
The calves all marked with shipping tags
It should be like drivin' with a map.

Now these calves have many tags, orange, blue and white
It takes a modern cowboy with a computer to do it right
The orange ones here, the blue ones there, a pen for each colour
The whites are for the government guys, they don't know one
from the other.

The liner arrives right on time and backs up to the chute
A whole year's work is loaded up, the gates all shut tight
The auctioneer tomorrow will try with all his might
For enough money to pay the bills when Ueli gets home tonight.

—Dec, 2002

Memories

It was down by the creek
As he watered his mare
He saw the little green frog
With the poker-faced stare.

He heard a voice in his head
It said, "Sir if you dare
Rub my tummy just right there
I've got something wonderful I'd like to share."

As he touched that frog
The air seemed to glisten
He thought he heard Mother
And he paused to listen.

She said, "Hello son, I see you're well
Your Dad's here with me, stop a spell
It's a long, long time since we were together
I see you kept farmin' in spite of the weather."

His vision cleared and there they stood
Hand-in-hand as they always would
The mare raised her head, looked all around
She had heard my dad make a familiar sound.

Sometimes in the country there's a magic time
When the Lord lets you glimpse a long-ago time.
All of a sudden, the frog gave a leap
Landed with a splash in the middle of the creek.

Sometimes in the country you have a vision so clear
Of someone you love, someone you hold dear
From deep in your heart, you've forgotten you had
A tucked away picture of your mother and dad.

Whitecroft

Mom and Dad went back to ranchin'
In the spring of forty-three.
The old doc had said with a shake of his head
Sure, looks like your son's gonna' get T.B.

We'll go back to the ranch to give him a chance
This cowboy and schoolteacher wife.
Back to the land, where we began
To build a ranch and a better life.

My Dad he was a butcher
And a cattle buyer too.
He bought cattle for the slaughterhouse
From Ashcroft into the Cariboo.

My Mom had been a teacher
In her younger days.
It would help to pull them through
When there were bills to pay.

So, he quit his job and sold the house
We pulled out on a rainy day.
The old Ford car was loaded for bear
We were finally on our way.

They left the big city with all those bright lights
To chase the Canadian Dream.
To have a big ranch out in the hills
Near those mountains, fields, and streams.

We'll just sit on the porch and watch the cows grow
Through those lazy summer days.
Up to their bellies in lush meadow grass
The dream we all share in so many ways.

The house was old with holes in the floor
The pack rats came in under the door.
With hammer and nails, paint, paper, and brush
Mom made it a home for all of us.

The pipes were all plugged
And the stove wouldn't draw.
We built up the wood pile
With an old crosscut saw.

When hayin' time came
Grandpa said, "Let's get goin'.
Time to hitch up the team
Let's get on with the mowin'."

The Indians came up with wagons and kids
To help with the hayin' like they always did.
They camped on the meadow, down by the creek
They usually stayed for six or eight weeks.

With horses and rakes, pitchforks and sloops
The work went fast till they went to Kamloops.
"The wife she needs groceries and I need beer"
After two or three weeks that was all you could hear.

After scratchin' your head, go down to the jail
You'd gather em' up and be payin' their bail.
Four days had gone by but they'd had their fun
They'd come back and work 'til the hayin' was done.

Paddy and Bonnie were Joe Seymour's dream
They made the old mower sing like the queen.
Baldy and Queenie, they pulled on the rake
The stack horse was Barney, it was all he could take.

A neighbour named Eva sold us a cow
For butter and milk and cream on our chow.
She was the first cow whose tit's I did pull
Then she kicked the damn bucket when it was near full.

That cow set the pattern for the rest of my life
When I sat down to milk there was sure to be strife.
She'd swing her old tail, shiver and shake
And hold up the milk I wanted to take.

When Eva was gone, Blossom came into my life
By now I had three kids and a city-bred wife.
I kept a 2 x 4 handy to help with the chore
Our personalities clashed like never before.

The last one was Valentine, raised from a calf
I let her calf suck and just took half.
If those kids would milk it wasn't so bad
But it was plain to see they were smarter than Dad.

When the kids got older, I told them my plan
You milk the cow or we'll get it from a can.
Now the bucket sits rusty out by the tree
The kids are all grown, now they drink tea.

Gramp's old horse, Candy, taught me to ride
He gave me a mare, Sox was my pride.
She took me to school and all over the place
On the way home the dogs we would race.

Mom was my teacher at that little school
Ten kids she taught the golden rule.
She read us stories and taught us to add
She showed us the world wasn't all bad.

We took the cutter to school one day in deep snow
All dressed up warm in blankets and fur.
We left the house with a snap and a jerk
Mom fell out of the cutter but wasn't hurt.

I dragged her a ways in that fluffy white snow
She looked like a grizzly bear fresh out for a blow.
She sputtered and stuttered, I felt like a fool
The day I dragged the teacher to school.

When I was about twelve, I got my first gun
Groundhogs and gophers were kept on the run.
One day in the house, unloading with care
I shot a hole in the ceiling: it gave me a scare.

Mom at the sink with her back to the show
I looked at the ceiling, there was no place to go.
She felt the back of her head and turned with a roar
I saw the look in her eye and got out the door.

"What in hell's going on" and Mother didn't swear
I knew I was lucky to get out of there.
From then on, I unloaded out in the woodshed
That's the story of Mother, nearly shot in the head.

I passed out of grade eight, she said that was fine
It's correspondence now for year number nine.
I made it to twelve studyin' at home
One year in town was the end of the line.

Jack Loveway and Dad gathered yearlings to brand
Jack Brady was plowin' that rich bottom land.
It came to an end that sunny May Day
The Lord touched our father and took him away.

Grief overwhelmed us as we laid him to rest
This cowboy and butcher, one of the best.
We must go on through strife and storm
A few years later "Whitecroft" was born.

The Forgotten Home

As you travel on the highways across our great land
An old house catches your eye down in the cottonwood stand
It stands forlorn and forgotten as you drive over to see
You wonder who the people were that planted these
majestic trees.

A hundred years have passed since he came here with his wife
From far away these people came to build a better life
They plowed the sod to plant their grain and struggled to survive
Through winter storm and summer heat they beat the odds
and thrived.

Through good crop years they got ahead, paid off the
government loan
They built this home that stands here now, but they are all
long gone
Sons and daughters carried on; they called this house their home
Three generations lived in this house; it was the family throne.

This house has rung with laughter and shared the family tears
As each generation came along and some left to meet their peers
Great Grannie planted all these trees and tended with loving care
Each one here now, the saskatoon, the cottonwoods, and the fir.

If these trees could talk and tell the tales of all that they have seen
Of those that lived in this old house, nearly hidden by the trees
Of children grown in this happy home and now all gone away
Of tears and joys and laughter in those bygone days.

How proud they were when it was built to keep them from
the cold
But now this relic from the past endures after the land was sold
The cottonwood trees whisper in the breeze and sing their
eternal song
Of hopes and dreams, now memories of times long past
and gone.

—Feb. 2003

My Silver Rose

Some Roses last and some fade away
But the Rose of my dreams is here today
Life has been kind, we both know it's true
A love like ours just happens to a few.

Fate brought us together many years ago
The gods smiled on us, I know it is so
This Rose from the city I chose for a wife
She came to the ranch, embraced country life.

Three children we raised, me and my Rose
How proud we were as we watched them grow
Now we're grandparents and time marches on
We've seven grandchildren to watch carry on.

Now her hair is turning silver, this Rose of mine
There's a line on her brow, but her eyes they still shine
Still full of the love that she's given to me
It's amazing how lucky one man can be.

As I stand here now and look back on my life
How lucky I was to choose a Rose for my wife
Through all the years our love has been true
To my SILVER ROSE, MY WIFE, HOW I LOVE YOU.

—Feb. 19, 2003

The Long Waltz

Many years ago, when I asked you to dance
You were very reluctant, but you took the chance
As I put my arm around you, and we took those first few steps
I knew I'd found my girl, which led to promises kept

As we danced that first waltz together
In the hall by old Heffley Creek
I knew I'd love you forever
As your shining hair brushed by my cheek

Through all my life I've had my Rose
You have helped me along the way
It's my turn now to help my Rose
Till we can waltz another day

I know you know I share your pain
As you shared mine so steadfast
I'll help you to recover, so we can waltz again
To that same old melody, so haunting from our past

The band still plays that tune, from down in Tennessee
We will hear it forever dear, as you dance through life with me
Our hair has turned to silver, as the music ebbs and flows
We will dance a little slower now, as on and on it goes

This dance isn't nearly over
Just pause to catch your breath
Now lay your cheek on my shoulder
I'll hold you while we rest

I still love to put my arm around you
And listen to the sound of the band
We will still waltz through life together
I know we are both in HIS hand.

—Written for Rose when she had
knee replacement surgery April 10, 1993

Tough Times

The long hot summer of two thousand and three
Is one that will linger in our memory.
The winter before was mild and nice
With not much snow and a little bit of ice.

As spring came along it was a farmer's dream
When the calves hit the ground, the grass turned green.
The sun shone bright early in May
Soon all were busy with the first crop of hay.

But trouble was brewing, it was called B.S.E.
Soon the price of those cows was down to your knee.
The border was closed, you couldn't sell a cow
But the cowmen optimistically said we'll get through somehow.

The sun it shone bright and hot every day
There wasn't enough water for the second crop of hay.
The range dried up, everything turned brown
More trouble came to us from someone in town.

A discarded cigarette started a blaze
Soon the sky was filled with a smoky haze.
The town of Louis Creek went up in smoke
The sawmill went too and most people's hope.

Another careless smoker started the Strawberry fire
It burnt all the fence posts and just left the wire.
Soon the power went off as the poles crashed down
Then all in the country were evacuated to town.

They registered us all at Sport Mart Place
So, they knew where we were and that all were safe.
Boiling smoke and flying ash filled the air
It almost seemed that God didn't care.

The flames consumed all in their path
Sagebrush, trees, wild animals, cows, and rancher's grass.
The firefighters came from all across the land
To fight this fire and make a stand.

On the ground and in the air they all worked together
Through terrible conditions and 38-degree weather.
The flames were insatiable; they had a life of their own
Soon smoke filled the valleys and covered the town.

The fire threatened Rayleigh, it came really close
Then over the hill to skirt Seven-O and burn up some hay.
And on to Cold Creek, burning everything in its way
Cows and calves, deer and bear, timber and fence
Nothing was spared wherever it went

Then off to the east, near Niskonlith Lake
Another lightning fire on land that was baked.
The heat and the wind drove this fire wild
It acted like a really spoiled child.

Down to the river, threatening the town of Chase
It flew in minutes to the mountain's base.
Back on itself, then up to the hills
Burning cabins and timber, it followed its own will.

McGillivray Lake and Sun Peaks Resort
Were all in danger at the last report.
Men and machines in the air and on the ground
Fought long and hard and somehow found
The strength and courage to make a stand
'Til mother nature relented and gave a helping hand.

Cooler temperatures, a few clouds, and some showers
Allowed the crew a little time to tame nature's power.
The fires died down, the smoke is gone, devastation remains
But nature with all its power will make it green again.

Soon winter's snow will cover all that was destroyed
Sleep now, await the spring and hopes will be bouyed.
This is "Next year's country" like the old cowboy said
"Get back on your horse, there's better days ahead."

—Summer 2003

Our Golf Gang

There's something strange about golfers
Now take the case of Al and Dee
If she'd listen to what he tells her
She'd have a better score than me.

There's something strange about golfers
That's a fact that we all know
After hitting those little white balls
Where does your common sense go.

Gary and June are the same way
He says to her, "It's your turn to pay"
"Not on your life cause I'm your wife
The contract says you must pay."

He sets up the ball upon the tee
He sets it there very carefully
Takes his club and sets up the drive
But the ball sure acts as if it's alive.

John R. and Elsie, now there's a pair
Seriously, both with white and red hair
John M. and Jimmy R. with the beard
John's jokes are getting worse, as we all feared.

After settin' up the shot in a professional way
Ninety percent of the time it goes its own way
Over the fence or into trees
If it isn't wet, it's in with the sand fleas.

Cory W. and Audrey, two ladies with class
They'd have a good score if they stayed on the grass
Rob tops his drives, but they roll like hell
Pappy Jack's the pro, proves that age will tell.

Our puttin's the same, we eye it with care
We do practice strokes, while our partners all stare
A light tap sends it off, they grin on the sly
A voice from above says, "Gord, you went by"

Velma and Rose look after the shoppin'
To get back for lunch keeps them hoppin'
Jack and Rob are glad to see them as they join our bunch
Because they have the money to pay for the lunch.

There's curly-haired Bill and Helen, sometimes
She joins us for coffee and Bill spins the lines
These old bus drivers and farmers that gather to play
We're thankful to be here on this bright sunny day.

It's only a game, we all say with a grin
But it sure would be nice if the damn ball went in!

—Christmas 2003

A Tear in Your Eye

The old rancher sat on his horse real still
Near the gate of the corral, on a little round hill.
He was counting his cows as they went by
There was just the hint of a tear in his eye.

For fifty-plus years he had counted them by
From a few scraggly cows, under the wide-open sky.
Memories flooded back as he watched them go by
That's why today, there's a tear in his eye.

He had struggled to survive, with his new bride
To build up his ranch for his family, his pride.
With his dreams and hard work, he reached for the prize
But today there's a hint of a tear in his eye.

A runaway horse had claimed his first son
But the pioneer spirit made him go on.
With his wife and three children, "We will still get by"
But there's still the hint of a tear in his eye.

As the years passed by and the children grew
The boys became cowmen, and the girl went to school.
She married and moved to the city, as time went by
That's why there's the hint of tear in his eye.

The second world war claimed son number two
In a far-off land, he was a hero, that's true.
With his wife and one son, "I know we'll get by"
That's why there's the hint of a tear in his eye.

Their hair turned to silver as that herd grew
"It's time to take over, son, it's all up to you.
Make us all proud, with your wife by your side"
So today there's the hint of a tear in his eye.

His son rode up the hill to stand by his dad
As the last of the herd went round a bend.
"Don't worry Dad, watch your grandsons ride by"
And he reached up and brushed a tear from his eye.

"I can recall all the trials mother and I have been through
But today when we're done, I pass the whole herd to you.
There's a lifetime of work in this herd that pass by"
No wonder there's the hint of a tear in their eyes.

The two of them stood on that little round hill
Beneath the wide-open sky, as cattlemen will.
The dreams are passed to each generation, that's why
Sometimes you'll see a tear in their eye.

— 2003

My Sister

My sister is skilled in the culinary arts
Her bread is delicious and so are her tarts
She's had lots of practice, she's cooked for years
Her cakes and her pies brought many to tears.

Then there's roast beef, and gravy that's thick
With turkeys and chickens, she had a special trick
She had lots of practice with a family to feed
A cook is essential for a ranch to succeed.

Through all those years her mistakes were few
Like the time she tried to pass off the really burnt stew
We loaded our plates, prepared for the feast
It wasn't like her bread, when she'd forgotten the yeast.

She'd doctored it up with spices and such
To hide the taste, but it didn't do much
The dog didn't mind, he seldom had such a feed
He is man's best friend in a time of need.

One time, building fences way far from home
With a pack horse, we left early to get the job done
About half the job done, we were feeling the crunch
So just about noon we settled down for lunch.

Sandwiches and coffee soon restored our trust
Now and again, I threw the dog a crust
But the cookies were strange, little round balls
Dates and crispies and coconut, that seemed to be all.

They smelled real good, so I took a bite
Had to crunch down harder, with all my might
There was no way, I couldn't make a dent
If I had false teeth they would have been bent.

So, I threw it to the dog, he grabbed it with glee
He chewed and chewed, then looked up at me
"It tastes real good," he seemed to say
"I hope there's just one or I'll be here all day."

We got the job done and got home just at dusk
'How did it go?" sister asked both of us
"We got the job done and ate all our lunch
But those little round cookies were just too much"

"They kept the dog busy," I said with a grin.
"That's mistake number 2, but that's not a sin
For all those good meals we've had through the years
I thank you my sister, you deserve three cheers."

—Dec 2003

The Great Canadian Dream

So, you want to be a rancher and ride the open range
Don't you think the urge is weird or maybe even strange?
The great Canadian dream is to have your own spread
Own a couple of horses and cows, just a few head.

The dreams of most city folk, as they struggle with their life
Counting up their money, talkin' to the kids and wife
"We've nearly got enough to tie up that their ranch
Now's the time to do it, kids, we gotta' take the chance."

"We'll get a mortgage at the bank and scrape up all our bucks
The dream is ours, we're ranchers now with all the rancher's luck"
They moved out to the country where the air is fresh and clear
The first lesson that they learned was the difference between
cows and steers.

The road to the ranch was dusty and potholes quite a few
They had been there last summer and just remembered the view
It had been muddy and slippery with puddles the size of lakes
When they got to the front gate their car still had the shakes.

The radiator was blowin' steam, the motor had hiccups
"The first thing that we should do," he said, "is buy a new pickup"
They moved their things into the house, kicked out the rats
and mice
"It shouldn't take you too long, dear, to fix it up real nice."

The wallpaper hung from the ceiling, smoky and torn into strips
And when she turned the tap on it gurgled a couple of drips.
"It won't take long honey, I'll have it all shipshape"
She thought of the home that she'd left and said,
"Dear, it's almost more'n I can take"

A couple of weeks of real hard work, it started to look like home
As she put up the curtains and said with a sigh,
"It's very nearly done"
Her hubby had cut some firewood and got the water to run
She still had trouble with the kitchen stove, the dampers, lids
and such.
It gobbled the wood, burnt the beans and the biscuits they
weren't much.
But youth and vigor overcame it all, in a month she was
learnin' how
To cope with every crisis and smooth the bumps to where
they'd go.

Two dogs they got to chase the cows, from the auction yard
To fetch them home and chase them away, now that shouldn't
be too hard
Now those old cows were pretty smart, they soon could fool
the dogs
They'd crawl the fence and push the gates and be standin' in
the yard
Wrapped in the clothesline and paw the garden
where she had worked so hard.

"Those god damn cows are sure a pain," she's sure learned
how to swear
As she cinched up the saddle on her sweet brown mare
She chased the cows into the field where he was pickin' rocks
"Here's your cows," she yelled at him, "that big one's wearin'
your socks!"

By the end of June, things were looking good, the spring work it
was done
"We'll take the cows to summer range, have a couple days of fun"
The morning dawned clear and bright, he smiled as he rode out
the gate
This is what he'd dreamed of and said, "Honey ain't this great"

"We'll join the neighbours around the bend and head on up
the hill"
He'd forgot about the traffic, gates, and the cows obstinate will
They crawled into the brush and stood there, the dog wouldn't
chase 'em out
It wasn't long before he was startin' to sweat and all he could do
was shout.

The old cowboy that was helpin', he spoke softly to his dog
A couple of nips and he grabbed the tail, the cows left in a fog
The secret of this cowboyin' you better learn it now
"There's sure is nothin' to it if you're smarter than a cow.

They rode over the range and had a wonderful day
However, it was back to the work of makin' hay
The tractor wouldn't start and the haybine was busted
He meant to fix it last year and now it was rusted.

Another day lost with skinned knuckles and pain
It was all running smoothly then it started to rain
When the showers were over, he got one field ready to bale
A thunderstorm came up, then it started to hail.

He turned it 5 times tryin' to dry it somehow
And muttered to himself, "I'm glad I'm not a cow."
He worked all that summer to put up his crop
A couple of bales were good but most of it was not.

As he pushed the last bale into the stack
He could hear the cows comin', on their way back
He sorted the calves and hauled them to town
At the auction the buyers said, "Sorry the prices are way down"

Maybe next year we'd have better luck
We'll just have to get by with our rusty old truck
Winter came in with a bang. It was minus forty-two
With shots for the heifers and supplements they finally got
them through.

January, February, and on into March, the winter it hung on
"I'll be glad to see spring come when all the snow is gone"
Calvin' started with a bang, the first one it was dead
He's up to his armpits in another, lookin' for the head.

The mud was startin' to dry up, he was getting used to pain
Then it snowed for 2 full days before turning into rain
He finally got them all calved out, they were lookin' really fine
Then scours hit, the calves got sick. It pushed him to the line.

With pills and needles in each hand he won this battle too.
It takes a little more than luck to pull you suckers through
This all happened years ago, he's really smarter now
He's up there on a level with the old boss cow.

Adversity and pain have made him a better man
He's won those many battles on his piece of land
Determination and true grit are all it takes it seems
To triumph and realize the Great Canadian Dream.

—2003

Through The Mist

Rose and Rob, with each passing day
Are showin' their age it's sad to say.
The years go by like pages in a book.
The spirits still there, they just change the look.

In '56 when they were wed
The future was bright as they looked ahead.
The ranch called "Whitecroft" was home to us all.
Jack, Vel and Mother, we all heard the call.

We cleared up the land for growin' more hay.
More cows was the word, we'll make it pay.
There were tractors and balers, rakes and trucks
Shops and barns a new house for us.

The guest ranch was started to help pay the bills.
That's when the kids started skiing those hills.
Civilization was changin' our way of life
It wasn't the same as when I wed my wife.

The ranch it was sold to Real Estate Men.
The dreams are gone of "what might have been."
We still live on the land in a much smaller way
And gaze through the mists to an earlier day.

Sox

She was the daughter of a thoroughbred
With class in every line
Clear of eye and clean of limb
With white socks on her feet behind.

When three days old her mother died
She was left here all alone
But the hired man found the pair
And took the baby home.

She would have died, but the hired man tried
A bottle of fresh cow's milk
She started to thrive and came without fail
Soon started to drink her milk from a pail.

I was ten years old about this time
When my grandpa took me aside
"Every boy needs a horse," he said to me
"The filly is yours to ride."

She took me to the school each day
And waited patiently till three
When free at last, we raced home fast
My dog, my mare, and me.

That sorrel mare that's part of me
A boyhood dream, now a memory
Many foals she gave me, each one a gem
I see my sorrel mare in each of them.

My grandpa was right, as he worked on his chew
Ridin' 'em bareback makes a rider of you.
Now sixty years later, I find a picture in a box
Of that little sorrel mare, that I called "Sox."

—March 2004

Gathering the Eggs

Living on the ranch we all had chores
The women did some and the men did more
Like milking the cows and cleaning the barn
It was all part of life then, back on the farm.

The girls worked in the garden and raised the chicks
The boys split the wood and made kindling sticks
Lighting the fires in the early morn'
To boil the kettle and get things warm.

Things went well 'til that day in the spring
From out in the hen house screams did ring
While gathering the eggs from the community nest
The girls had competition from a real smelly guest.

They had lifted the lid and there to behold
A black and white pussy cat, lookin' real bold.
Shiny black hair with a white stripe down the middle
He was stampin' his feet like he was playin' a fiddle.

The hens were upset when they slammed the lid on that box
They flew to the roosts with many loud squawks
The girls left the hen house with unlady-like haste
From the dust they stirred up you'd swear they were chased.

It was no competition, the skunk grinned as they ran
There were no eggs today for the old fryin' pan
He ate five or six, then licked off his chin
Then ambling off, said, "I may come back again."

"It would be real nice if you put a window in that nest
So, I could look out and see if I was havin' guests
It startled me so and I just have to shiver
When I realize how close I was to pullin' the trigger."

—March 2004

Old Ford Car

I'm an old Ford car with a piston ring
Two rear wheels and one front spring
Have no fenders, seat, or plank
Burn lots of juice and am hard to crank
Carburetor busted halfway through
Engine misses hits on two.

I'm three years old, be four in the spring
I got shock absorbers and everything
I got a rocking and wobbling gate
Takes two boards to guide me straight
I run in high but quit in low.

The devil himself couldn't make me go
Got lots of speed if you turn me loose
I burn either gas or tobacco juice
My tires all off been run on the rim
But I'm a damn good Ford for the shape I'm in.

Our Golf Buddy

Gordon was a real nice guy; on that we all agree.
Dressed for golf one sunny day, he left us suddenly.
But he still plays along with us and has quite a lark
For his spirit roams the greens at McArthur Park.

The spirit of Gordon Wilkie roams the Mac Park greens
So, when his old buddies play there, there's five on the team.
He often took a rose to Shelley when he went to pay his fee
Then we all gathered at the door to head out to the tee.

At number one as you tee off
The water gods do call.
A nice smooth swing, then you hear him scoff
As the ripples radiate from that drowning ball.

"Keep your eye on the ball, let the club do the rest,
soon you'll be playing along with the best."
Up on the green you're getting near at last
"Take it easy on that putt Al, see, you've gone right past."

At number two, Bill tees up right.
It's supposed to go high and land real light.
He sends the ball upon its way
But the river claims his ball today.

"Aim it true at number three, it's got a way to go"
Gary's shot is over the fence because he sliced it so.
You see, he shot a brand-new ball, it's to get his goat,
No matter how you try, the damn things never float.

At number four, we've been here before, it rolls right to the grass
But on the grass, it rolls right past, like we've often seen.
"It's not in the sand, you're lucky Jack, you still can make par."
But Gordy's words can still be heard, "Don't hit the ball too far."

On number five, there's choices three
It's either water, thorns, or in the trees.
The green it beckons, right in the centre
And Rob's third shot couldn't be better.

On six, on both sides there's lots of water.
We've warmed up now, it's getting hotter.
"Don't mind the water, pretend it's not there
Gord will make sure your ball lands somewhere."

Up on the hill at tee number seven
You should make it in three, but it ends up eleven.
Keep your eye on the ball, keep your head down
There's a chuckle on the wind, you know Gord's around.

We move on to eight, cross over the bridge
Hit over the water but it lands on the edge.
After going for another ball, Cory sets up again.
It's that voice that she hears that same old refrain.

On number nine it's a straight shot to the flag.
Here Jack shows us how, you should hear him brag.
Up on the green, we're all near the cup at last
Gord's voice is heard by all, "Carefully now, don't go past."

—August 2004

My Belt Buckle

Of all the stories there are to tell
This one may make you chuckle
A cowboy's friend from start to end
It's about my old belt buckle.

It's been with me for sixty years
A friend through life's struggles
A longhorn's head on nickel plate
Adorned my new belt buckle.

A proud possession for a boy of ten
As it graced my cowboy kings
The leather belt was way too long
But time will change some things.

It was shiny and new as I threaded it through
The loops of my working jeans
As I pulled it tight with all my might
I felt just like a cowboy, a boyhood dream come true.

Through school years and countless chores
To my working years, bales, tractors and more
On fishing trips and hunting, also chasing cows
On the ride all these years and still with me now.

It's worn around the edges, from the constant wear
The longhorn head worn away, the background it is bare
Through all the years, silently you've done your work just fine
Doing your job every day, that old belt buckle of mine.

—2004

You Went Right Past

I first met Gord many years in the past
A really good friend, what more could you ask
We drove school buses on Tod Mountain Road
Braved all kinds of weather to pick up our load.

We'd all go for coffee to talk about our trip
About how slippery the road or the car in the ditch
How this kid or that touched our heart in different ways
As we played a small part in each kid's day.

He was like a grampa to all those small kids
He bandaged their bruises and listened to what they did
He went to the concerts to show that he cared
About those young lives we were honoured to share.

Then came the day, the end of the trip
Retirements ahead, Gord, here's your pink slip
Now Gord was a golfer of some renown
When he drove that ball, it would land and bound.

He'd saunter up and chip on the green
The nicest shot you've ever seen
With putter in hand, he'd take up his stand
Line up that shot and with a firm hand.

Stroke that ball a little too fast
A real nice putt, Gord, "but you went right past"
Now you've gone on ahead, Gord, so make a tee time
And when that day comes, we'll meet you at nine.

We'll tee up again Gord and St. Peter may ask,
"Why do all your friends say, 'Gord you went right past.'"

Gerry

A new mechanic came to district twenty-four
Soon Gerry Halbert was out on the floor.
With wrenches and skill, he did his best
To help keep the fleet running, he was up to the test.

He moved to the office to look after "Skylark"
A dispatcher was he, and he made his mark.
For his was the quiet voice on the radio
The voice of Skylark we all came to know.

Between Shirley and Frank, the guy in the middle
Our problems were his, a gigantic riddle.
Out on the road in all kinds of weather
When we called for help, somehow, he made it better.

We called on Gerry when the fights got too bad,
For girls pulling hair and those "mad as hell" dads,
Irate principals, teachers that were late.
In spite of us all, most kids turn out great.

Through all those years he was surely blessed
With a wife like Bonnie, who didn't protest
The mornings and nights that he was on call.
For mechanics and drivers, he looked after us all.

One more move put him in charge of the fleet
Stait became dispatcher and took over his seat.
Now that retirement's here, we all wish you the best
Gerry, may your years ahead be truly blessed.

—January 2004

Fifty Years Later

When Lou was finished high school
She moved out to the "Y"
To spread her wings and make her way
Independent was Lou, and still is to this day.

A couple of jobs along the way, then a move to Orange Crush
She met a trucker "Stan," he really gave her a rush
In a couple of years they married, she was hard to convince
Now fifty years have gone by since she took the chance.

Several moves along the way, problems they overcame
They met them all, they learned to play the game
Two babies they were blessed with, one God took away
Christina came to brush the tears, bring sunshine to their days.

The brother-in-law that bugs her, she has come to accept
She is still a little nervous of what he will do next,
This verse is for both of you, we wish you all the best
May the years that are to follow, be full of happiness.

—June 2006

Hole in One

Gordon and God were having a beer
God looked down and said—look here
Those friends of yours are out to have some fun
Maybe we should give one a hole in one.

I gave one to Cory a couple of years back
Those other three are Al, Rob and Jack
I'll bring up some wind by the 3rd hole
A little adversity will be good for their soul.

The wind brought some clouds, angry and black
By hole number six they were on their way back
From the southwest the wind came with a blast
I could hear Al mutter, "Jack you went past."

"Shades of old Gordy," he said with a grin
As he tapped it again and it finally went in
Rob hit his three times, he had another miss
"I'm sure Willkie's got his hand in this!"

On seven Corey and Jack leaned into the wind
They shot to the left, they must have sinned
Al shot to the right. "I'll fool him," God said with a grin
"Right about now I'll stop the wind."

Rob teed up his ball, leaned well to the west
Gord's words of encouragement made me try my best
That wild west wind took the ball on its chin
Rolled onto the fairway, hit the green and rolled in.

Now look at that, see what you've done
Here on the seventh "a hole in one"
I couldn't believe it as I walked up and looked in
There it was nestled in the hole by the pin.

I could hear Gord chuckle through the wind's blast
"For once in your life you didn't go past."

—Mar.13, 2001

Corrie

Corrie, our golf buddy has crossed the divide
She is now with Gord on the other side.
The family she left will carry on
And cherish the memories of times bygone.
It's all right now if you shed a tear
For a mother and grandmother who loved you all dear.

Gord welcomed her there with wide open arms
"Let's go out to the club for a couple of rounds.
I'm so excited to see you now that you're here
Our clubs are all ready, let's get going my dear."

"You were always ready, no matter the weather
No worries up here, the sun shines forever.
We play on the clouds, the best fairways of all
You never have to look for your lost ball.
When the water up here swallows your ball
Just part the water, no trouble at all."

"These fairway clouds are always great
When you drive the ball, it always goes straight.
Every putt goes true, into the cup at last
No need to say, 'Corrie, you went right past.'"

Corrie's travels with Gord down life's long road
With family and friends, leaves us memories to hold.
We will miss you Corrie, friend, mother, and wife
For the part you played in our life
God speed to you when you reach heaven's door
May you rest with the Lord forevermore.

—July 2007

Our Wells Gray Panama Trip

Lynda is our guide, on this Wells Gray trip
Roland made her come so there would be no slip
From Kamloops and Kelowna and Okanagan towns
We all met her at Merritt and gathered around.

The bus drove the Coq with a lunch stop at Hope
It kept us going till we got on the boat.
It's a ship not a boat, she was quite frank
If you call it a boat, you'll be walkin' the plank.

She got us on board like an old mother hen
It was at the dining room we saw her again.
For eighteen days they fed us like kings
With time on shore to buy baubles and things.

Astoria, San Diego, Cabo San Lucas
Vallarta, Acapulco, Huatulco, and Chiapas.
Puntarenas and Panama, the most fascinating day
Then Cartagena Columbia, were some stops on the way.

Each day at sea as we travelled far
She set up shop in the Ocean Bar.
She listened to our stories and laughed at our jokes
She sure knows how to handle us old folks.

Our thanks to Holland America, the captain and crew
The Wells Gray staff that made this dream come true.
To all our new friends, as this trip nears its end
Let's give our thanks to Lynda, our own mother hen.

—Oct. 15, 2007

Our Special Guide

Lynda, Lynda, we love you
Your one hellu'va guide
It's a good thing we had you with us
Or we'd have been left on the other side.

From the ship to Seattle by airplane
Your smile just led us on
The border guard didn't have a chance
It must have been those short-legged pants.

On the bus as we travel the Coq
Through the rain and sleet and snow
All of us folks behind you
Will follow wherever you go.

So, thanks to all the folks at Wells Gray
For a super trip
If you don't promise to guide us next time
We ain't going to give you a tip.

—Oct 2007

So Long Jack

So long Jack, it has been a long ride
Down the trail of life
Since you met my sister
And made her your wife.

We became as close as brothers
As close as two guys can get
It's hard to believe it's over seventy years
Since the two of us met.

It's been a hellu'va ride Jack
Down the trail of all those years
Through all kinds of weather
Lots of laughs and a few tears.

After Dad left us, we swallowed our loss
We built up the ranch, with Mom as the boss
We plowed up the land, and baled the hay
Raised our families together, those were heady days.

The long rides together, those freezing-cold days
Those were the times that made our memories
Our families grew and prospered, went on their way
Retirement came for both of us, it was time to play.

We played golf with all our friends
Travelled from north to south and east to west
We will part for now, but it's not the end
It's time for you to go on to heavens rest.

You have done your part in this life, so go on Jack
Ride those heavenly fields and trails
You will meet those who have gone before you,
Along through heavens vale.

There's good days ahead, of that we are sure
The grass will be tall and the water pure
The sun will shine on mountain and glen
Enjoy it Brother, we will meet again.

—April 29, 2008

Uncle Jack

My uncle Jack was always near
Like a second Dad, to dry our tears.
After lunch, we would go down to the shop
To meet him there, and maybe hippity hop.

He would send us to Auntie for Juicy Fruit gum
To keep us occupied and on the run.
He'd say one for Frank, one for me
One for mostest Mary, one for me.
But "Jack" that's not fair, you have two
That's because I'm bigger than you.

Then there was Shannon, she helped him fix
Jesus' "Jack," this damn thing's a bitch.
Get me a wrench, stay out of the grease
That's how Uncle Jack looked after his niece.

Soon our play would turn into a fight
I'll count to three, then give it all your might.
One and two, if we didn't stop, he ki-yi and dance,
Soon we'd have to laugh, that's our Uncle Jack.

Summertime haying, riding on the sloop
Picking up bales, part of the group.
The big water bottle, we would all have a drink
Then need to go pee, behind a bale, don't peek.

"The Battle of New Orleans" was his theme song
We would sing it together as we rode along.
While feeding the bale flakes one by one
Watching the cows come on the run.

Skiing was also part of our life too
Uncle Jack and us kids made up the crew.
When we got bigger, and his grandchildren came
He skied with us all, made it a game.

Spearmint gum, ju jubes and toffee candy,
He teased us all with anything handy.
He enjoyed us all and our babies too
As the years passed our love for him grew.

Time goes by as we all know
The good Lord tells us when we must go.
The laughter and joy you brought to our life
Enriched us all, eased some of the strife.

The memories we have, will live through the years
We will cherish them always, even the tears.
We will meet again, we all know
When and where? "YOU JUST NEVER KNOW"

The Old Man

He paused at the door and looked back once more
At the home they had built together
Young they had been, barely out of their teens
So many years, laughter and tears, they thought they'd be
there forever.

The government bet 10 bucks—they would give 'em the land
for free
If they could build a home, and clear in a year, acres three
They started in a sod shanty, and tackled the land with zest
In three years, they got the title, they had passed the test.

The children came one, two, three, more room was needed, plain
to see
It took them years to build this home, it seemed there was no rest
Things were looking pretty good, they farmed and logged and
sold the wood
The family grew and prospered, for years that seemed the way.

Strong sons and daughters helped ease the work, more each day
Then came the day, the kids went away to work in the big town
She said "Slow down Dad" your back's achin' bad, it's startin' to
get you down
Just do the chores, you can't do more, it's time to take a rest.

Just sit on the deck in your rocking chair, and enjoy the farm
we made
You worked so hard all those years, years I would not trade
But when he woke one morning, his wife had passed away
The sun was gone from his life, replaced by clouds that day.

So, he sold the farm, and all they had built, money he had a pile
To live an empty life, without his wife in a retirement home
in style
It wasn't what he had dreamed of when he'd worked his
fingers sore
But there was no alternative, as he paused at the kitchen door.

As he took his hat from the deer-horn rack, the memories came
once more
His son was there at the bottom of the stair, to help him to
the car
With one last look at the meadows, he left the door ajar
He paused and seemed to listen; he heard her voice from afar
Go on Dad, get in the car, the home where they're taking you
isn't far.

Here you can live out your days, with no worries along the way
The trouble is my friends are gone; this is where old folks stay
These people are all strangers, city folks, to them I have nothing
to say
I miss you so, but I know, in time we will be back together.

We'll be young again, on heaven's range, where there is no
bad weather
No cares or worries will haunt us there, the grass is lush and tall
The cows will come home all alone, we'll see them all this fall
So, he shut the door, and got in the car with his memories packed
up neat
He could see his wife was waiting, like she was just up the street.

—July 24, 2008

The Homesteader

He was just a farmer
Hoeing the stubborn ground.
He liked the open spaces, solitude
Didn't want many folks around.

So, he took his wife and family,
Out into the wild west.
With stalwart sons and daughters,
He fought and did his best.

A piece of land and a cow or two
Freedom was all he sought.
Those men and women of bygone times
They built this land we've got.

It's up to their sons to carry on
Though the family farms nearly done.
The spirit is strong, but will it survive?
On the foundation that they've begun.

Those sons grew up to be cowmen
Built ranches and herds to last,
But government shattered their outlook
A hundred years was all it took.

And people forgot where they get their food
The sweat and tears that make it good.
Now it comes, in a cellophane wrap
No taste, no flavour, just tastes like crap.

The stubborn sons of the few who are left,
Those who share their forefather's dream
Will stand the pressure, and do their best
To feed the world, on the land that is left.

—2008

Old Jake

Old Jake was a cowboy from long ago
He had ridden more ranges than we'll ever know,
He had ridden more horses from the age of three
That's why all the room between his knees.

As time goes by cowboys' knees get bowed
From all those bronc's that he's rode.
There comes a time when chasin' cows is done
A new line of work has to be found in town.

He sold his saddle and hung up his spurs
Put on his best clothes and combed his hair free of burrs.
He applied at the drugstore, selling ointments and stuff,
The first day on the job went smooth enough.

'Til the fat lady waddled in all sweated up
Said, "Son l need some powder for places that rub."
Right this way, said old Jake, "Walk this way
I've got the right powder to take the itch away."

So off he went, bow legged down the aisle
"This powder will make things alright in a while,"
Behind him she waddled said, "Son, if l could walk that way
l wouldn't need powder on these hot days."

—Aug 24, 2008

Two Broken Spurs

The homestead barn stood forlorn
Alone on the deserted farm,
The broken door lured me on
To memories of those long gone.

Two old brushes and a curry comb
Told of the care he took,
Of his horses after a day long ride
I paused and turned to look aside.

To a box nailed on the wall
Just beyond the single stall,
Hidden there, deep in dust
Two broken spurs called out to us.

Two broken spurs, they weren't worth much
But the owner had a careful touch,
He laid the pieces there with care
Knowing someone, would find them there.

Just made of iron, but with loving care
Out of a pitchfork, he shaped them there.
With fire and hammer they took shape
Those iron spurs that he could make.

The rowels and buckles he added to
The leather straps to go under his shoe.
He was just a poor homesteader makin' his way,
A ghost from the past that I awoke today.

I took those pieces home with me
With a modern torch I set them free,
New buckles for the leather straps
Fit on my boots, under my chaps.

I used them for years, as I chased my cows
Those iron spurs, that I brought back to life.
Now they hang on my wall, I'm done for now
With those old iron spurs from another life.

The tales they could tell from their time with him
Are gone now, and those memories grow dim,
When he forged those spurs, with such care.
I wish I had known him and been there.

—Nov. 2008

My Silver Belly Stetson

My silver-coloured Stetson hangs on the peg for all to see
It was the last Christmas present that my mother gave to me
The colour is some faded now, and it's lost that new hat look
I took it to the hatter once, he steamed and reshaped the block.

But when I wore it on a ride, the old shape came right back
It felt so good when I put it on, it was like a friend came back
That hat was my companion, checkin' newborn calves in spring.
I wore it at the brandings, and weaning fall calves when they
came in.

It's been to all the cattle sales, could spin some real tall tales
Like buying pregnant heifers in a Walachine wintery gale.
They had a fire burning that we all huddled round
Waiting for the auctioneer to start that rhythmic sound.

It was 40 below and blowin' when the auctioneer started to call
The bidding was mighty brisk, none of us wanted to stall
Then there were the summer rides to put the cows up high
It rained so hard I nearly died, there sure was no blue sky.

Though there were lots of sunny days that were like heaven
on Earth
Early mornings and late sunsets, we got our money's worth.
It went on our wagon trips and, on the ninety's cattle drives,
It even saw me bucked off, once or twice for exercise.

Through 40 years I wore that hat, it was just a part of me
But now it hangs on that peg, it's pensioned off like me
I don't ride the bush no more, those ridin' days are done
All I have is memories, of days and rides long gone.

—December 2008

Dagmar and Springfield Ranch

Politics and wars can shape our lives
Then fate steps in and stirs in some chance.
So it was, with Dagmar and Frank
They met, married, and carried on the dream of
Springfield ranch.

They begat three children to carry on the dream
Then fate again, stirred in more chance.
The third generation was destined it seems
To carry the dream of Springfield ranch.

Grandchildren grow up to continue
What was started so many years ago.
This changing world may baffle you
But the lessons you taught are showing through.

No one knows what secrets the future holds
But one hundred years of history we have seen unfold,
Your grandchildren will guide with a sure hand,
The future of Springfield ranch, this blessed land.

So, Dagmar on your 90th birthday
Relatives and friends wish you well
May Springfield ranch continue to prosper
There are many more chapters of this story to tell.

—July 2009

Summer Ride

It was a cold day in August, the rain was pouring down
The hayin' it was stopped, too much water on the ground.
Some cows they needed moving, up to some better grass
So, I loaded up my saddle horse and headed up the pass.

They were crowded round the cattleguard, sayin' let us go home
So, I got on my saddle horse, with my Dry-za-Bone.
The rain it was peltin' down so hard, I could hardly see
Those cows were sure ornery, they didn't want to listen to me.

I finally got 'em headed out, to the cut block out the back
When my hat started leakin' it ran right down the crack
My pants they were soaked right through, especially where I sat
That Dry-za-Bone it worked okay, but it didn't cover my hat.

I was feelin' kinda' sorry when a truck came up the hill
My wife had come to rescue me, she knew I'd had my fill.
That city girl that I had wed, drove right up by my side
"I was just wonderin'" she said, "WOULD YOU LIKE A RIDE"

—June 6, 2012

Old Boots Old Saddle

My old boots are worn and scuffed at the heels
They been around too long, l know how they feel
I oiled them and polished them and put them away
Thinking I'd wear them some other day.

My saddle is oiled, and put on the rack
Along with my chaps and some other tack
My hope is someday, a gentle horse will decide
To come and get me for one final ride.

The horses from my past crowd my memories today
l know l will see them, as I pass on my way
This life has been good, there is nought to deny
As we all go to pasture, up in the sky.

—June 6, 2012

Old Folks

Old George and his wife Samantha
Were getting along in years
They still enjoyed pretty good health
But their memories had slipped a few gears.

She sat in her favourite old rocking chair
She was knitting a shawl for herself
Old George rose from his nest on the couch
And laid his book back on the shelf.

He looked at the clock on the mantelpiece
And turned to his wife and said
"Dear, would you like something to eat
Before we trot off to bed."

"Why yes, a dish of ice cream would be nice
With some chocolate on top, just a smidge
But write it down George, I know you'll forget
By the time you get to the fridge."

So, he toddled off to the kitchen
On his time-worn, crooked old legs
And he came toddling back in half an hour
With a plate of bacon and eggs.

The old girl lay down her knitting
She sighed, "George you're a pretty good host
Do you remember, I told you to write it down
Don't you see, you've forgotten the toast."

Rob My Dad

Farewell Dad!
Let the wildflower in you
Grow wild in heaven above
No longer can we see you

Or touch your hard-working hands
We feel your presence in every poem
Written here on Earth
What a great life you lived.

Not always knowing your destiny
From school in Kamloops to
The abrupt turn of going to UBC
To running a cattle ranch in the wild west.

Destiny brought you together
To dance 66 years with your Rose
Family you created just the two of you
Children, grandchildren, and beautiful grandbabies too!

They will pass on your legacy.
Go on and dance with Mom
You can rest now, Dad
At 90 your work is done!

Love you Dad

—Rosemary, 2023

About the Author

Robert W. White was born in Vancouver, B.C. After he started showing signs of tuberculosis as a child, his family moved to the interior of British Columbia in the hopes the hot, dry climate would improve his health. Upper Louis Creek valley was a new experience for Rob. There were barns, guns, old farm machinery, and lots of room to roam. After meeting and marrying the Rose of his dreams, Rob settled in a small house on a ranch.

Rob liked to ski, fish in the creeks, play golf, and of course write poetry. He spent his whole life in Kamloops and the Upper Louis Creek Valley. He had three children: Frank, Rosemary, and Shannon, who are all married and have families of their own. Rob's sister Velma was married to Jack Brady, and had two children, Barry and Brenda, who are also married and have children of their own.

I dedicate this book to all my family and friends that I love so much. May you all live life to the fullest, stay safe and LOVE each other every day.

Printed in the USA
CPSIA information can be obtained
at www.ICGtesting.com
LVHW041113010424
775857LV00001B/83